99 Positive Steps
Toward Achieving 100%,

the next step is YOURS!

99 Positive Steps
Toward Achieving 100%,
the next step is YOURS!

Prophet Ramon

authorHOUSE®

AuthorHouse™ LLC
1663 Liberty Drive
Bloomington, IN 47403
www.authorhouse.com
Phone: 1-800-839-8640

Published by AuthorHouse   08/01/2013

ISBN: 978-1-4817-7041-5 (sc)
ISBN: 978-1-4817-7040-8 (e)

Library of Congress Control Number: 2013911691

Any people depicted in stock imagery provided by Thinkstock are models, and such images are being used for illustrative purposes only.
Certain stock imagery © Thinkstock.

This book is printed on acid-free paper.

Because of the dynamic nature of the Internet, any web addresses or links contained in this book may have changed since publication and may no longer be valid. The views expressed in this work are solely those of the author and do not necessarily reflect the views of the publisher, and the publisher hereby disclaims any responsibility for them.

Foreword

"To everything there is a season, and a time
to every purpose under heaven."

Some people are seasonal and we attempt to
make them permanent.

Some people are seasonal and we attempt
to make them permanent. This leads to
frustration and resentment when the season of
that relationship has passed and no purpose or
reason for the continuance of the connection
can be realized. Pray for the ability to discern
what God has placed in your life for a season.
This will allow you to find purpose in the
time that the relationship exists, without the
expectation of a permanent bond.

Live Life Liberally,
Literally with Love
and Laughter.

Introduction

This book is to be used as a daily guide to reflect on the events of the day as well as prepare for tomorrow. Read the step for the day and then make notes on how you put the step into action. Above all, be honest. If you cheat, you are only cheating yourself.

Today is the first day of the rest of your life. You only get one chance to make a good first impression . . . . act like you know!!!

Dedication

My Children
Christie Lee Kreider
David Ramon Weaver, Jr.
Dante Murclay Weaver

Special Thanks to Buttercup

STEP ONE

What good thing can I do today? To whom a kind word can I say? How can I show the love of God in action? —By using my hands to help, my voice to heal, and my heart to love.

Today, I commit myself to take one (1) positive step forward!

STEP TWO

A charge to keep I have: my God to glorify; a never dying soul to save and fit it for the sky.

To serve this present age, my calling to fulfill—oh let my will be lost in Thine and do Thy blessed will.

Today, I commit myself to take two (2) positive steps forward!

STEP THREE

This is the day that the Lord has made. I will rejoice and be glad in it. Make the most out of what you have been given: the breath of life, the blessing of health, and bounty beyond measure.

Today, I commit myself to take three (3) positive steps forward!

STEP FOUR

Celebrate life! It is a gift, not to be taken lightly. Each new day offers an opportunity for enlightenment. Push beyond the limits that have been set before you—you can be more than you imagine if you will do more, give more, and love more.

Today, I commit myself to take four (4) positive steps forward!

STEP FIVE

Whoever it is, He loves you. Whatever it is, He helps you. Whenever it is, He is prepared.

Wherever it is, He goes there. Why-ever it is, He doesn't care. However it is, favor isn't fair.

Because that's just how He is!

Today, I commit myself to take five (5) positive steps forward!

STEP SIX

God gives us new mercies every day like sunshine which guides us along our way. He is faithful and He is true. Right now you can depend on God. I wonder, can God depend on you?

Today, I commit myself to take six (6) positive steps forward!

STEP SEVEN

You are a bright light that shines in a world of darkness. Let your light shine before mankind, so that they may see the goodness of God working through you, and thereby, be inspired to give glory to our Father who is in Heaven. Is your light turned on?

Today, I commit myself to take seven (7) positive steps forward!

STEP EIGHT

There is a way that is right: a way that removes all darkness with a marvelous light, a way of truth that tells no lie, a way that lives and will never die. Jesus is the way, the truth, and the life. He stands at the door to your heart. Open it and let Him come in.

Today, I commit myself to take eight (8) positive steps forward!

STEP NINE

We are instruments of praise, curiously, wondrously and intentionally designed and created for the purpose of praising God. Within every second of every minute of every hour of every day we are given, through the gift of life, another opportunity to give God praise. Can you think of just one reason to give God praise?

Today, I commit myself to take nine (9) positive steps forward!

STEP TEN

Now faith is made of hope and proven by the unseen. Take a step in faith and see if God will do as He promised; to lead and guide you in the way that is right and to do for you, in you, and through you what no other power can do.

Today, I commit myself to take ten (10) positive steps forward!

STEP ELEVEN

God is our refuge and our strength. He will open his hand wide to those who call upon His name. For I was young and now I am old yet I have never seen the righteous forsaken nor his seed beg for bread.

Today, I commit myself to take eleven (11) positive steps forward!

STEP TWELVE

Have no fear when dark clouds rise or when suddenly the skies turn gray, for into each life some rain must fall, and without rain there is no growth and without growth, there is no maturity and without maturity, there is only adolescence.

Today, I commit myself to take twelve (12) positive steps forward!

STEP THIRTEEN

Yesterday is past, tomorrow is yet unborn, and all that is real is today. So seize this day. Do all you can, while you can, for whomever you can, because this may be your last day to do so.

Today, I commit myself to take thirteen (13) positive steps forward!

STEP FOURTEEN

If you think there is no God, then you have invited calamity into the path of your life. You may think of a path that is right, but it will lead to isolation. Seek the Savior while He may be found and His love will never leave you lonely.

Today, I commit myself to take fourteen (14) positive steps forward!

STEP FIFTEEN

There is only one God: the giver of every good and perfect gift. He is faithful and He is true. It is no secret what God can do. What He's done for others, He will do for you too.

Today, I commit myself to take fifteen (15) positive steps forward!

STEP SIXTEEN

For as the heavens are higher than the earth, so are His ways higher than your ways, and His thoughts than your thoughts. If you think that God will only do things your way . . . think again.

Today, I commit myself to take sixteen (16) positive steps forward!

STEP SEVENTEEN

If you have faith the size of a mustard seed, you can tell a mountain to move and it will move. And nothing shall be impossible unto you. All things are possible if you only believe.

Today, I commit myself to take seventeen (17) positive steps forward!

STEP EIGHTEEN

I've had some good days and I've had some hills to climb. But when I look back over my life and think things over—all of my good days, outweigh my bad days, so I won't complain.

Today, I commit myself to take eighteen (18) positive steps forward!

STEP NINETEEN

I've heard the story of King David, and I've heard of Daniel in the lion's den. I've heard of Job with his afflictions and how they all kept the faith until the end. So when all hope seems to fail, that's when God's power will prevail and I know that prayer changes things.

Today, I commit myself to take nineteen (19) positive steps forward!

STEP TWENTY

Behind every dark cloud is a silver lining, so seek the bright side of life when troubles try to weigh you down. Lift up your head and look to the hills from whence cometh your help. All your help comes from God.

Today, I commit myself to take twenty (20) positive steps forward!

STEP TWENTY-ONE

Everything must change. Nothing stays the same. There are not many things in life you can be sure of, except, rain comes from the clouds, sun lights up the sky, and hummingbirds do fly. All the days of my appointed time will I wait until my change comes.

Today, I commit myself to take twenty-one (21) positive steps forward!

STEP TWENTY-TWO

When you walk through a storm, hold your head up high and don't be afraid of the dark. For He has not despised nor abhorred the afflictions of the afflicted neither has He hid His face from them; but when we cry unto Him, He hears us. God cares for me and for you.

Today, I commit myself to take twenty-two (22) positive steps forward!

STEP TWENTY-THREE

The thief only comes to steal your joy, kill your body, and destroy your soul. Jesus comes to give you life more abundantly. Don't let the devil ride.

Today, I commit myself to take twenty-three (23) positive steps forward!

STEP TWENTY-FOUR

Oh give thanks unto the Lord for He is good. You may not have a car at all, but remember brothers and sisters, you can still stand tall. Just be thankful for what you got.

Today, I commit myself to take twenty-four (24) positive steps forward!

STEP TWENTY-FIVE

I lift up mine eyes unto Thee, O Thou that dwellest in the heavens. Up above my head I hear music in the air and I know there must be a God somewhere. God is real in my soul.

Today, I commit myself to take twenty-five (25) positive steps forward!

STEP TWENTY-SIX

Search me Lord. Turn the light from heaven on my soul. If you find anything that should not be, take it out and strengthen me. I want to be right, I want to be saved, I want to be whole.

Today, I commit myself to take twenty-six (26) positive steps forward!

STEP TWENTY-SEVEN

Trust in God and be not ashamed, for He will not let your enemies triumph over you. In all thy ways acknowledge the Lord and He shall direct thy path. I will trust in the Lord always.

Today, I commit myself to take twenty-seven (27) positive steps forward!

STEP TWENTY-EIGHT

God is the source and the strength of my life; whom shall I fear? He has not given me a spirit of fear, but of power, of love, and of a sound mind. When God is with me and moving through me, the world may rise against me, yet, I will stand triumphant.

Today, I commit myself to take twenty-eight (28) positive steps forward!

STEP TWENTY-NINE

I heard the voice of Jesus say, "Come unto me and rest. Take my yoke upon you, for my yoke is easy and my burdens are light." Jesus, the load lightening legend.

Today, I commit myself to take twenty-nine (29) positive steps forward!

STEP THIRTY

Jesus Christ represents the fullness of God in bodily form. All things were made by Him, and without Him, nothing was made. Be careful for nothing, but in all things through prayer and supplication make your request known to God.

Today, I commit myself to take thirty (30) positive steps forward!

STEP THIRTY-ONE

I am free, thank the Lord, I'm free: no longer bound, no more chains holding me. My soul is rested; oh what a blessing to me, thank the Lord, hallelujah, I'm free. Stand fast in the liberty wherewith Christ has made us free and be not entangled with the yoke of bondage. He whom the Lord sets free is free indeed.

Today, I commit myself to take thirty-one (31) positive steps forward!

STEP THIRTY-TWO

I am not ashamed of the gospel of Jesus Christ, for it is the power of God unto salvation for everyone that believes it. Since we have heard the report of the Lord, and the rhetoric of men, who will we believe? I choose to believe the report of the Lord.

Today, I commit myself to take thirty-two (32) positive steps forward!

STEP THIRTY-THREE

The night is far spent, the day is at hand; let us therefore cast off the works of darkness, and let us put on the armor of light. God is light and in Him there is no darkness at all.

Today, I commit myself to take thirty-three (33) positive steps forward!

STEP THIRTY-FOUR

I will speak well of the Lord all of the time through the ups and the downs, the joys and the sorrows that fill this life. I have a blessed assurance knowing that there is nothing which can remove me from the love of God. In all things, I am more than a conqueror through Jesus Christ our Lord.

Today, I commit myself to take thirty-four (34) positive steps forward!

STEP THIRTY-FIVE

They smile in your face, but really they're trying to take your place, the backstabbers. But don't worry yourself over evildoers, nor over those who work against you—"Vengeance is mine," says the Lord. God has got your back.

Today, I commit myself to take thirty-five (35) positive steps forward!

STEP THIRTY-SIX

Rejoice in the Lord and be exceedingly glad. Shout with a loud voice and a voice of triumph, for God has made your enemies your footstools and brought you up out of a horrible pit. Establish your downsitting and your uprising. Our God is a Great God.

Today, I commit myself to take thirty-six (36) positive steps forward!

STEP THIRTY-SEVEN

Bless the Lord, O my soul and all that is within me, bless His holy name. Praise God from whom all blessings flow. When praises go up, blessings come down.

Today, I commit myself to take thirty-seven (37) positive steps forward!

STEP THIRTY-EIGHT

Be faithful over a few things and God will make you the ruler over many things. The steps of a good man are ordered by the Lord and he delights in its way. Faith is the buckle that fastens the belt of hope which holds up the pants of prayer.

Today, I commit myself to take thirty-eight (38) positive steps forward!

STEP THIRTY-NINE

Hear the voice of the Lord; attend to the words of His mouth. Ask and it shall be given you; seek and ye shall find; knock and it shall be opened unto you. So let him that has a mouth, speak; and let him that has an eye, see; and let him that has ears, hear; and let him that has hands, do; and let him that has feet, go. Obedience is better than sacrifice.

Today, I commit myself to take thirty-nine (39) positive steps forward!

STEP FORTY

I waited patiently for the Lord, and He inclined unto me and heard my cry. "Comfort ye my people," saith your God. Weeping may endure for the night, but joy comes with the morning light. The storm is passing over—glory hallelujah.

Today, I commit myself to take forty (40) positive steps forward!

STEP FORTY-ONE

Set a watch, O Lord, before my mouth; keep the door to my lips. He that keepeth his mouth, keepeth his life: BUT, he that open wide his lips shall have destruction. Remember: Watch your mouth.

Today, I commit myself to take forty-one (41) positive steps forward!

STEP FORTY-TWO

Thou are my everlasting portion, more than friends or life to me. All along this tedious journey, Savior let me walk with Thee. I say "unto Thee O Lord, Thou art my refuge and my portion in the land of the living."

Today, I commit myself to take forty-two (42) positive steps forward!

STEP FORTY-THREE

Use me Lord, in Thy service; draw me nearer, every day. I am willing to run on all the way. If I falter while I'm trying, don't be angry. Let me stay, for I am willing to run on all the way.

Today, I commit myself to take forty-three (43) positive steps forward!

STEP FORTY-FOUR

Blessed be the Lord my strength, which teacheth my hands war, and my fingers to fight: my goodness and my fortress, my high tower and my deliverer, my shield, and He in whom I trust.

Today, I commit myself to take forty-four (44) positive steps forward!

STEP FORTY-FIVE

Every day will I bless Thee; and I will praise Thy name forever and ever. Great is the lord, and greatly to be praised and His greatness is unsearchable. O taste and see that the Lord is good.

Today, I commit myself to take forty-five (45) positive steps forward!

STEP FORTY-SIX

Count your blessings. Name them one by one. Take the time to reflect on the good things that God has done for you: woke you out of slumber, secured mental clarity, and physical strength. Go to the ant thou sluggard, consider her ways and become wise.

Today, I commit myself to take forty-six (46) positive steps forward!

STEP FORTY-SEVEN

Since we are surrounded by such a great crowd of witnesses, let us run with patience the race that is set before us, looking to Jesus, the author and finisher of our faith, who endured all things, including death to ensure unto us, salvation that is secured. Jesus paid it all and all to Him I owe.

Today, I commit myself to take forty-seven (47) positive steps forward!

STEP FORTY-EIGHT

When I consider the heavens and the works of Thy fingers, the moon and the stars, which Thou hast ordered; what is man, that Thou art mindful of him? And the Son of Man, that Thou visiteth him? God is able to solve my problems. I only have to trust Him.

Today, I commit myself to take forty-eight (48) positive steps forward!

STEP FORTY-NINE

Allow the little children to come freely to Christ, for such is the kingdom of heaven. Except ye become as little children ye shall in no wise enter the kingdom of heaven. Jesus loves the little children, all the children of the world. Red, yellow, black, and white, they are precious in His sight.

Today, I commit myself to take forty-nine (49) positive steps forward!

STEP FIFTY

As for God, His way is perfect; the word of the Lord is tried. He is a way of protection to those that trust in Him. Please be patient with me. God is not finished with me yet. When God completes His work with me, I shall come forth as pure gold.

Today, I commit myself to take fifty (50) positive steps forward!

STEP FIFTY-ONE

Let us hold fast to the profession of our faith without wavering. And let us consider one another to provoke unto love and to good works. Speak kind words while they may be heard, so that someone may feel the joy that they bring.

Today, I commit myself to take fifty-one (51) positive steps forward!

STEP FIFTY-TWO

I once was alone and idle. I was a sinner too. I heard the voice from heaven, saying there is work to do. So I took the Master's Hand, and I joined the Christian Band. Now I'm on the battlefield for my Lord. Only you can do what is for you to do.

Today, I commit myself to take fifty-two (52) positive steps forward!

STEP FIFTY-THREE

Time is filled with swift transitions. One on earth unmoved can stand. Build your hope on things eternal. Hold on to God's unchanging hand. Man will fail, but God will never fail.

Today, I commit myself to take fifty-three (53) positive steps forward!

STEP FIFTY-FOUR

Hear my prayer, O God; give ear to the words of my mouth, for I will freely sacrifice praise unto Thee. I will praise Thy name, O Lord, for Thy name is good. God is good, all the time.

Today, I commit myself to take fifty-three (53) positive steps forward!

STEP FIFTY-FIVE

As for me, I will call upon God and the Lord shall save me. Evening and morning, and at noon, will I pray, and He shall hear my voice. Just a talk with Jesus can make things alright.

Today, I commit myself to take fifty-five (55) positive steps forward!

STEP FIFTY-SIX

In God I live, I move, and I have my being. In God I have put my trust. I will not fear what flesh can do unto me. I will not be afraid of what man can do unto me. I will trust in the Lord until I die.

Today, I commit myself to take fifty-six (56) positive steps forward!

STEP FIFTY-SEVEN

Awake, O my soul: awake, psaltery and harp. I myself will awake early. I will give thanks to you O Lord, for your kindness towers to the heavens, and your faithfulness to the skies. Rejoice in the Lord. Again, I say rejoice.

Today, I commit myself to take fifty-seven (57) positive steps forward!

STEP FIFTY-EIGHT

O come, let us sing unto the Lord; let us make a joyful noise to the rock of our salvation. Let us come before His presence with thanksgiving. Giving from your heart will produce getting with your hands.

Today, I commit myself to take fifty-eight (58) positive steps forward!

STEP FIFTY-NINE

O Lord, my God, when I in awesome wonder, consider all the world Thy hands have made. I see the stars. I hear the rolling thunder: Thy power throughout the universe displayed. Great is the Lord, and greatly to be praised.

Today, I commit myself to take fifty-nine (59) positive steps forward!

STEP SIXTY

There is nothing more precious than Jesus to me. Let earth with its riches be gone. I'm as rich as can be, when my Savior I see. I'm happy with Jesus alone.

Today, I commit myself to take sixty (60) positive steps forward!

SIXTY-ONE

From everlasting to everlasting Thou art God. You provide comfort to me when my heart is overwhelmed. Take my hand and lead me unto Thy way, for Thou has been a shelter to me and a strong tower.

Today, I commit myself to take sixty-one (61) positive steps forward!

STEP SIXTY-TWO

I love you Lord, and I lift my voice to worship you; O my soul, rejoice. Take joy my King in what we bring, let it be a sweet, sweet sound in Your ear. I have loved the habitation of Thy house, and the place Thine honor dwelleth. I exhalt Thee O, God.

Today, I commit myself to take sixty-two (62) positive steps forward!

STEP SIXTY-THREE

See to it that no one takes you captive through hollow and deceptive philosophy which depends on human tradition and the basic principles of this world, rather than on Christ.

Today, I commit myself to take sixty-three (63) positive steps forward!

STEP SIXTY-FOUR

He that dewlleth in the secret place of the Most High shall abide under the shadow of the Almighty. This is the year of obedience: a year to listen, to hear, and to do.

Today, I commit myself to take sixty-four (64) positive steps forward!

Step Sixty-Five

If you take one step, God will take two. There is no secret what God can do. If you go, don't worry about yourself. All you have to do is take a step. Step with love in Christ. The Lord will lead the way. Live with love and share God's love always.

Today, I commit myself to take sixty-five (65) positive steps forward!

STEP SIXTY-SIX

No one can serve two masters. Either you will hate one and love the other, or you will be devoted to one and despise the other; you cannot serve both God and man. Lord, I want to be a Christian in my heart.

Today, I commit myself to take sisty-six (66) positive steps forward!

STEP SIXTY-SEVEN

God be merciful unto us and bless us; and make His face to shine upon us. Let the people praise Thee O God; let all the people praise Thee. Bless the Lord, O my soul, and all that is within me bless His Holy name, for He has done great things.

Today, I commit myself to take sixty-seven (67) positive steps forward!

STEP SIXTY-EIGHT

If it had not been for the Lord on my side, tell me where would I be? Where would I be? He kept my enemies away. He made the sun shine through a cloudy day. He rocked me in the cradle of His arms when He knew I had been battered by the storm.

Jehovah-Rohi: The Lord God is our Protector.

Today, I commit myself to take sixty-eight (68) positive steps forward!

STEP SIXTY-NINE

A flower that blooms in May, the sunset at the end of the day, someone helping a stranger along the way: that's heaven to me. It doesn't have to be a miracle, for me to see, the goodness of my God, is everywhere daily. The children playing in the street, say hello to everyone they meet, even the leaves growing out on a tree: that's heaven to me.

Jehovah-Shammah: The Lord God is Present.

Today, I commit myself to take sixty-nine (69) positive steps forward!

STEP SEVENTY

May all those that seek Thee, rejoice and be glad in Thee and may they who love Thy salvation say continually, "May God be magnified."

Jehovah-Yahweh: The Lord God is our Salvation.

Today, I commit myself to take seventy (70) positive steps forward!

STEP SEVENTY-ONE

O God, Thou hast taught me from my youth and I declare Thy wondrous works. I am as a wonder unto many but Thou art my strong refuge. Thou shalt increase my greatness and comfort me on every side.

Jehovah-Gmolah: The Lord God is our Recompense.

Today, I commit myself to take seventy-one (71) positive steps forward!

STEP SEVENTY-TWO

Blessed be the name of the Lord our God who does wondrous things. His name shall endure forever. His name shall be continued as long as the sun and men shall be blessed by Him. All nations shall call Him blessed.

Jehovah-Tsidkenu: The Lord God is our Righteousness.

Today, I commit myself to take seventy-two (72) positive steps forward!

STEP SEVENTY-THREE

Whom have I in heaven but Thee? And there is none upon the earth that I love more than Thee, O God. It is good for me to draw near to God. I have put my trust in the Lord God that I may declare all Thy works.

Jehovah-Nissi: The Lord God is our Banner.

Today, I commit myself to take seventy-three (73) positive steps forward!

STEP SEVENTY-FOUR

Like a ship that's been tossed and driven, battered by an angry sea. When the storms of life are raging, and its fury falls on me. I look up and wonder why, the good things just pass me by, then I say to my soul, "Take courage and know, the Lord will make a way, somehow."

Jehovah-Jireh: The Lord God is our Provider.

Today, I commit myself to take seventy-four (74) positive steps forward!

STEP SEVENTY-FIVE

There is therefore now no condemnation to them which are in Christ Jesus, who walk not after the flesh, but after the Spirit.

Jehovah-Maccaddeshem: The Lord God is our Sanctifier.

Today, I commit myself to take seventy-five (75) positive steps forward!

STEP SEVENTY-SIX

Amazing Grace shall always be my song of praise, for it was grace that brought my liberty. I do not know, just why Christ came to love me so. He looked beyond my fault and saw my needs.

Jehovah-Shalom: The Lord God is our Peace.

Today, I commit myself to take seventy-six (76) positive steps forward!

STEP SEVENTY-SEVEN

There were ten men in the Bible days who had been sick for so very long. One day Jesus passed their way, and when He spoke, their disease was healed that day. But they all went on their separate ways, yet one returned and said, "Thank you Lord."

Jehovah-Rapha: The Lord God is our Healer.

Today, I commit myself to take seventy-seven (77) positive steps forward!

STEP SEVENTY-EIGHT

I will open my mouth in a parable. I will utter dark sayings of old: that the generation to come might know them, even the children which should be born; that they might set their hope in God and not forget His works.

Jehovah-Sabboath: The Lord God is our Lord of Host.

Today, I commit myself to take seventy-eight (78) positive steps forward!

STEP SEVENTY-NINE

So we Thy people and the sheep of Thy pasture will give Thee thanks forever. We will show forth Thy praise to all generations.

Today, I commit myself to take seventy-nine (79) positive steps forward!

STEP EIGHTY

Let Thy hand be upon all of creation and upon the Son of Man, whom Thou has made strong and full of courage. God always gives us a hand that is full of help.

Today, I commit myself to take eighty (80) positive steps forward!

STEP EIGHTY-ONE

Be ye strong in the Lord and in the power of His might. Put on the whole armor of God so that ye may be able to stand against the evil influence of the devil. We are fighting a Christian Warfare.

Today, I commit myself to take eighty-one (81) positive steps forward!

STEP EIGHTY-TWO

For our enemy is not made of flesh and blood but of the principles, policies, and powers of this world and the spiritual rulers of evil that exist in this dimension of time and space.

Rule Number One: We must KNOW who we are fighting.

Today, I commit myself to take eighty-two (82) positive steps forward!

STEP EIGHTY-THREE

Cover your body with the Armor of God; so that ye may be able to withstand the attacks from our enemies which are sure to increase in these evil days. And after you have done all to stand, you just stand.

Rule Number Two: We must be dressed properly in order to stand.

Today, I commit myself to take eighty-three (83) positive steps forward!

STEP EIGHTY-FOUR

The BELT of TRUTH: is the first piece of the Armor of God to be placed around the part of the body that is on either side of the backbone and between the ribs and the hips thus encircling the body.

Rule Number Three: We must gird up our loins in truth.

Today, I commit myself to take eighty-four (84) positive steps forward!

STEP EIGHTY-FIVE

The BREASTPLATE: is the second piece of the Armor of God to be placed on the chest of the believer, protecting the heart which holds the power to love and forgive. Let not your heart be troubled; believe in God.

Rule Number Four: We must put on the breastplate of righteousness.

Today, I commit myself to take eighty-five (85) positive steps forward!

STEP EIGHTY-SIX

The GOSPEL SHOES: are the third piece of the Armor of God worn on the feet of the believer. The steps of a good man are ordered by the Lord and he delighted in His way.

Rule Number Five: We must put on the preparation of the Gospel of Peace.

Today, I commit myself to take eighty-six (86) positive steps forward!

STEP EIGHTY-SEVEN

The SHIELD OF FAITH: is the fourth piece of the Armor of God to be placed on the arm of the believer, wherewith ye shall be able to quench all of the attacks from the enemy.

Rule Number Six: We must take the Shield of Faith.

Today, I commit myself to take eighty-seven (87) positive steps forward!

STEP EIGHTY-EIGHT

The HELMET: is the fifth piece of the Armor of God to protect the conscious mind and unconscious thoughts of the believer. Let this mind be in you: that was also in Christ Jesus.

Rule Number Seven: We must put on the Helmet of Salvation.

Today, I commit myself to take eighty-eight (88) positive steps forward!

STEP EIGHTY-NINE

The SWORD OF THE SPIRIT: is the sixth piece of the Armor of God. This is an offensive weapon and it is also a defensive weapon as well. It is comprised of the Word of God which has three distinct attributes: quick, powerful, and sharper than a two-edged sword.

Rule Number Eight: We must take the Sword of the Spirit.

Today, I commit myself to take eighty-nine (89) positive steps forward!

STEP NINETY

PRAYER: the seventh piece of the Armor of God and it is also one of the weapons of our warfare.

The effectual fervent prayer of the righteous bring both remedy and relief. There's power in prayer.

Rule Number Nine: We must put into practice the Power of Prayer.

Today, I commit myself to take ninety (90) positive steps forward!

STEP NINETY-ONE

SUPPLICATION: the eighth piece of the Armor of God. This is the ability to defend the needs of others and not simply yourself because the good that you do will come back to you.

Rule Number Ten: We must give a blessing, if we want to get a blessing.

Today, I commit myself to take ninety-one (91) positive steps forward!

STEP NINETY-TWO

WATCHING: the ninth piece of the Armor of God. The believer is to maintain a sense of readiness, focus, and determination. Let us be watchful and strengthen the thing that remains.

Rule Number Eleven: We must watch unto the coming of our Lord.

Today, I commit myself to take ninety-one (92) positive steps forward!

STEP NINETY-THREE

BOLDNESS: the tenth piece of the Armor of God. In Christ Jesus our Lord, we have boldness and access with confidence by the faith of Him.

Rule Number Twelve: We must come boldly unto the throne of grace, that we may obtain mercy, and grace to help in the time of need.

Today, I commit myself to take ninety-three (93) positive steps forward!

STEP NINETY-FOUR

When I lose my footing, Thy mercy, O Lord, holds me up. In the multitude of my thoughts within me, Thy comfort delights my soul. For the Lord is my defense and my God is the rock of my refuge. When I need shelter or when I need a friend, I can go to the Rock.

Today, I commit myself to take ninety-four (94) positive steps forward!

STEP NINETY-FIVE

O come let us sing unto the Lord; let us make a joyful noise to the Rock of our salvation. Let us come before His presence with thanksgiving and make a joyful noise unto Him with loud voices. Speak kind words while they may be heard.

Today, I commit myself to take ninety-five (95) positive steps forward!

STEP NINETY-SIX

The pride of man shall bring him low but honor shall uphold the humble in Spirit. There is no chastening of the Lord that seems joyous, but grevious. Nevertheless afterward it yields the peaceful fruit of righteousness unto them which are exercised thereby.

Today, I commit myself to take ninety-six (96) positive steps forward!

STEP NINETY-SEVEN

How much better is it to get wisdom than gold and to get understanding rather than silver! Pride goes before destruction and a condescending spirit before a fall.

Today, I commit myself to take ninety-seven (97) positive steps forward!

STEP NINETY-EIGHT

There is a way that seems right unto man, but the end thereof are the ways of destruction. Understanding is the well-spring of life to him that has it.

Today, I commit myself to take ninety-eight (98) positive steps forward!

STEP NINETY-NINE

Now unto Him, that is able to do exceedingly abundantly above all that we ask or think, according to the power that worketh in us; To the only wise God, our Father, be glory, majesty, dominion, and power; both now, henceforth, and forevermore.

Today, I commit myself to take ninety-nine (99) positive steps forward!

These are the 99 Positive Steps
Toward Achieving 100% . . . .
the next step is up to you.